LIFE
SKILLS

STUDY FOR SUCCESS

Tessa Phipps

Heinemann Library
Chicago, Illinois

Customer Service 888–454–2279

Visit our website at www.heinemannraintree.com

Edited by Harriet Milles, Megan Cotugno, and Rachel Howells
Designed by Philippa Jenkins and Hart MacLeod
Original illustrations © Pearson Education Limited
Illustrations by Clare Elsom
Picture research by Elizabeth Alexander and Maria Joannou
Production by Alison Parsons

Originated by Modern Age Repro House Ltd.
Printed and bound in China by South China Printing Company Ltd.

13 12 11 10 09
10 9 8 7 6 5 4 3 2 1

Library of Congress Cataloging-in-Publication Data
Phipps, Tessa.
  Study for success / Tessa Phipps.
     p. cm. -- (Life skills)
  Includes bibliographical references (p.) and index.
  ISBN 978-1-4329-1360-1
  1. Study skills. 2. Learning strategies. I. Title.
  LB1049.P446 2008
  371.3'0281--dc22
                          2008020257

Acknowledgments
We would like to thank the following for permission to reproduce photographs: ©Alamy **pp. 7** (Angela Hampton Picture Library), **17** (Jupiterimages/ Brand X), **19** (Andrew Compton), **24** (Corbis Super RF), **25** (Corbis Premium RF), **31** (Jacky Chapman), **41** (Jeff Greenberg), **45** (TMI); ©Corbis **p. 21** (Thinkstock); ©Getty Images **pp. 22** (Iconica/ ColorBlind Images), **39** (Blend Images); ©Masterfile **p. 5** (Peter Griffith); ©Photolibrary **pp. 43** (Hans-Peter Merten), **47** (Alain Le Bot/Photononstop); ©Rex Features **p. 48** (United National Photographers); ©Science Photo Library **pp. 15** (David N. Davis), **26** (Andrew Lambert Photography).

Cover photograph of teenage boy behind a stack of books reproduced with permission of © Punchstock (Brand X Pictures).

We would like to thank Tristan Boyer Binns for her invaluable help in the preparation of this book.

Contents

Some words are printed in bold, **like this**. You can find out what they mean by looking in the glossary.

Why the Big Fuss?

Study skills—the art of knowing how best to approach your schoolwork in order to get good grades—sounds like a pretty simple idea. You may think, "I've been studying for a long time, so why would I need to learn new study skills?" The answer is as simple as the idea: times have changed since you first learned how to study.

BRAIN POWER

In recent years scientists have learned more about the brain and how it works. **Psychologists** have learned how people can improve their learning and memory skills by using visual and audio clues. In this book, you will learn about a number of modern methods you can use to improve your study skills and help you get good grades on test day!

Independent thinking

The thinking on how best to remember things has changed—and so have you. You are no longer "spoon-fed" ideas, as you were when you were younger. Now you are expected to work independently, research things for yourself, analyze, be creative, come up with your own ideas, and formulate your *own* opinion.

The transition between the generous support of grade school and the virtual independence of college is a gradual process. With guidance and practice you will develop the skills

Getting it **Right**

Television advertisers are in tune with scientific research on how the mind works. They know that they have a captive audience that is in a relaxed and positive state of mind while watching a favorite TV show. In addition, they know how to make a lasting impression on their viewers by appealing to their emotions with catchy tunes and strong visual images.

you need in order to cope with these developing demands. Planning your work and studying efficiently can make a big difference in the pressure you may experience when you are making that transition.

We all learn in different ways, so in order to work effectively you need to find out the very best method to suit *you*. This book will help you identify which learning method is the best for you. It will also show you how to improve your performance by dealing with practical matters such as **time management** and creating a good working environment. Finally, you will learn how to improve your reading skills, tackle essay writing, and prepare for tests and exams.

How well you remember information can have a big impact on what you achieve in school—and beyond!

Getting it Wrong

In the past, people thought the best way to remember things was by repeating them over and over again. Not only can this be boring, but we now know that repetition on its own is not the most efficient way of getting information to stick in our heads.

Get Organized!

Taking a more strategic approach to your studies means that you will need to have all the right tools. You do not have to spend a fortune, and these tools will save a lot of time and effort when it comes to doing well in your studies.

TAKING STOCK

You can make a fresh start any time, but at the beginning of the school year or before the start of a new semester, take stock of your supplies to make sure you have everything you need. That way you will not have to worry about what you need when the pressure builds up over the course of the school year.

Planning ahead

Once you have the basic supplies, use a wall chart to get the big picture of what to expect in the coming weeks or months. You can either buy a wall chart or make one yourself using wide sheets of paper, a roll of paper, or even the back of a roll of wallpaper.

Use your wall chart as a planner, and start by putting in all the important dates for the semester and the year. That way you can see at a glance what is coming up and plan ahead accordingly.

What to put on a wall chart:

- Semester dates and holidays

- Assignment deadlines for different subjects

- Deadlines for projects and papers

- Test and exam dates

- Clubs and leisure activities

- Games and sports competitions

- Outings, field trips, lectures

- Time for research

• CHECKLIST •

You may need the following equipment to help your studies:

- Ring binders with different colored dividers for each subject
- Lined and plain paper. You may also like to choose different colored paper for different subjects.
- Punched plastic pockets to fit in your ring binder
- A selection of colored notebooks for various uses—for example, for assignments, for vocabulary, and for website addresses. Notebooks with a spiral binding are particularly useful since you can tear out pages you do not want. Address books can be used to write out vocabulary in alphabetical order.
- Index cards and a card holder
- Sticky notes and adhesive clay
- A calculator, protractor, or compass, if needed
- An English dictionary, **thesaurus**, and foreign language dictionary, if you are studying a foreign language
- Pens, pencils, erasers, rulers, colored pencils, pens, and highlighters

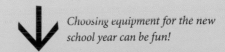

Choosing equipment for the new school year can be fun!

COMPUTER RESOURCES

Computers play a significant part in everyday life, and also in your school studies. You may have a computer you can use at home. If not, you should have access to computers at your school or local library. Whatever your situation, find out where and when you can have regular access to a computer to help you achieve your goals. And remember, a computer is a tool designed to help you, not to run your life.

Email

Use email for communicating with your classmates when organizing study groups or to ask questions when, for example, you have forgotten what has been assigned. Some teachers prefer the use of email for sending important messages or when sending in work for grading. That way your teacher will have the document and can correct your work by **tracking** changes. This marks errors in red in the document so that when it comes back to you, you will be able to see clearly where you have made mistakes.

USB memory sticks

Memory sticks are extremely useful for schoolwork, because you can use them on your computer at home and at school. This means that you can work on any given project in both places.

Calendars

Besides using your big-picture wall chart, you can use a computer to help you plan your workload. If you have regular access to the same computer, use a diary feature to chart your project deadlines and study plans, using software that is probably already available on your computer.

If you do not have calendar software, you can create your own calendar online. (See page 52 for useful websites to help you.)

Getting it Wrong

It may seem like a good idea, but don't be tempted to rely on your cell phone as a diary. You may get distracted by an incoming call or text, or you may lose your phone. Also, cell phones generally have to be switched off in class and in the library—and you must never take a cell phone into an exam room. This might cause you a major penalty.

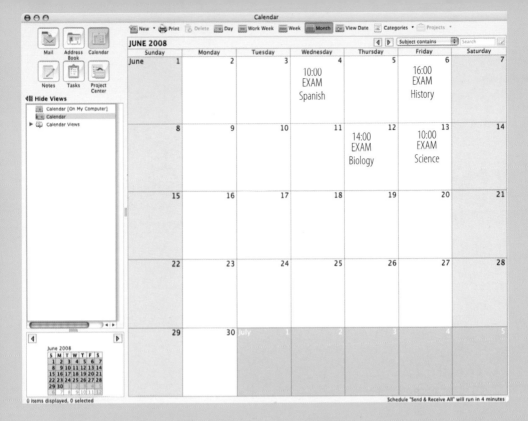

JUNE 2008

Sunday	Monday	Tuesday	Wednesday	Thursday	Friday	Saturday
June 1	2	3	4 10:00 EXAM Spanish	5	6 16:00 EXAM History	7
8	9	10	11	12 14:00 EXAM Biology	13 10:00 EXAM Science	14
15	16	17	18	19	20	21
22	23	24	25	26	27	28
29	30 July	1	2	3	4	5

0 items displayed, 0 selected   Schedule "Send & Receive All" will run in 4 minutes

Use a computer calendar so you can see what you need to do quickly and efficiently.

Filing systems

If you have regular access to the same computer, set up a clear filing system so that you can readily access the information you need. For example, create a folder for each subject within a master folder clearly labeled and placed on your desktop. Alternatively, place files you use regularly in your "favorites" box, or, if you are using an Apple computer, place them in the "dock".

If using your own computer, remember to install and maintain a security system to protect your work, regularly back up your work, and remove what you do not need so your computer does not become overloaded.

Even if you do not have regular access to the same computer, you can set up and maintain files for free online. Run a search for "free online storage" to find a place to store your files. (See page 53 for useful websites to help you.)

9

Spreadsheets

There are a variety of spreadsheet programs you can use for anything involving calculations. Spreadsheet software can also produce graphs from the figures you input. Spreadsheets are an invaluable tool to help you with your studies. In math or business studies you might, for example, be asked to draw up tables illustrating the difference in sales figures for a particular product between winter and summer.

After a geography field trip, George needed to demonstrate what he had discovered about coastal erosion. He used PowerPoint to create a presentation including photographs, facts, and figures. The software gave his presentation a "wow-factor" far beyond what his scrawled notes and handful of pictures would have done.

You can give your work a professional finish by presenting it in Excel.

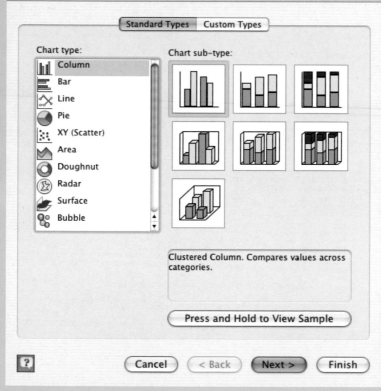

THE INTERNET

You are a lucky generation! Your parents may have had computers to help them with their schoolwork, but your grandparents certainly did not. Today, you can research just about anything on the Internet. Although there may be limits set on the types of websites you can access at home or in school, the Internet itself has no overall governing body. It is simply a system that links computers all around the world, with Internet service providers, or **ISP**s, bringing it into homes, schools, and businesses.

Streamline searches

When looking things up on the Internet, try to be as specific as possible, because otherwise you might be overwhelmed with information. Search engines normally have help pages that give you tips on how to best get the results you are after.

Common search tips include using the word *OR* to find pages that include either of two search terms or *AND* to find pages that include both terms.

If you only want to view pages about a specific person, place that person's full name in quotation marks. If you want to search for a number range, use two dots, as in 1900..1920.

If you want to search for a word and its **synonyms**, place a tilde sign (~) before the word you are searching on.

Back up your facts

Never assume that what you find or read on the Internet is accurate. Some facts and figures may be out of date. When doing research online, always find a second source to back up any facts that you find. Another good idea is to use educational or government websites (.edu or .gov), since the information there is likely to be more accurate than information on commercial websites. When using an Internet source, always keep track of where you got your information.

Tips for safe surfing: TIP

There is no doubt the Internet can be helpful with your studies, but remember to use it safely and *sensibly*:

- Talk to your parents or guardians about the sites you are using.

- Keep all details about yourself private.

- Keep your password secret.

- Don't send anyone your photograph and *never* agree to meet anyone you have chatted with online, but don't know.

The Great Brain

Your brain is the most amazing powerhouse. It allows you to walk, talk, laugh, cry, read, make friends, and above all, think. All thoughts, ideas, and memories are stored in the brain. In addition, the brain is the body's nerve center, which controls movement and our senses.

INFORMATION PROCESSOR

The brain is made up of over 100,000 million cells called **neurons**. At any one moment your brain is receiving about 100 million pieces of information, which are fed by your sensory organs—the eyes, ears, nose, tongue, and skin—through your **nervous system**. This network of neurons uses chemicals and the body's form of electricity to enable you to communicate, think, and feel.

Your changing brain

Scientists have known for a long time that the brains of babies grow at great speed until the age of about six or seven. Recently scientists have also found that the part of the brain that controls planning, memory, organization, and mood starts to grow in teenage brains just before **puberty**.

As the brain matures, teenagers learn to reason, develop more control, and make better decisions. Make the most of your growing brain by caring for it and treating it with respect.

DID YOU KNOW?

Brain-teasers, **trivia**, and **riddles** are three tools people can use to keep their minds sharp. See if you can solve this riddle:

> I am a protector.
>
> I sit on a bridge.
>
> One person can see right through me, while others wonder what I hide.
>
> What am I?

(Go to page 50 to check out the answer!)

"If I had to live my life again I would have made a rule to read some poetry and listen to some music at least once a week; for perhaps the parts of my brain now atrophied [wasted away] could thus have been kept active through use."

Charles Darwin, scientist and naturalist (1809–1882)

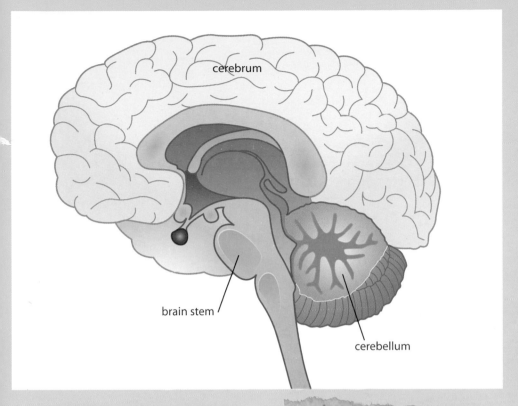

cerebrum

brain stem

cerebellum

 The largest part of the brain is the cerebrum, which controls vision, speaking, thinking, and your feelings.

Train your brain

The brain is a creature of habit. It learns how you react to things, and over time it responds to them automatically in the way it thinks you will respond. Your brain is like a muscle—the more you use it, the better it gets. Solving math problems, learning a language, doing crossword puzzles—any mental activity **stimulates** blood flow, strengthens your brain, and speeds up your thinking.

Getting it Wrong

If you watch a lot of television, you are also training your brain. Using your brain non-productively teaches your brain to behave in a non-productive way. Remember that just like "you are what you eat," your brain is what you do. If you use it non-productively, it will become lazy.

Energizing your brain

Glucose, which is produced in the liver, is the main source of energy for the brain. It is transported through the blood to the brain. There, oxygen burns the glucose to generate energy and provide the brain with the chemicals that enable brain cells to communicate with one another.

Exercise your brain and body

In order to help your brain function as effectively as possible, it is essential to get regular exercise, as this increases the amount of oxygen supplied to the brain. Clearly, the best amount of exercise varies from person to person, but experts suggest that a young person should exercise at least an hour per day.

Exercising refreshes the brain. It helps your brain to think more clearly, and as a result you perform better when you need to use your head.

Exercise will help you feel great, too! Exercise releases chemicals called endorphins and adrenaline into the brain (depending on the type of activity), both of which lift your mood naturally. This makes you feel happier and in a more positive frame of mind, which encourages you to tackle your studies more effectively.

Getting it Right

Your brain needs energy to work properly, and it is each person's responsibility to take care of his or her brain. If you want to make the most of your studies, it is important to get your brain in top condition. Get plenty of exercise, drink water regularly, and eat a well-balanced diet. Unlike muscles, the brain does not store energy, so it is important to regularly replenish it with **nutrients**. Eating regular meals that are high in nutrients will help keep your brain in top form. It is especially important to eat lots of fruits and vegetables, You should never skip breakfast, because this gives your body energy to keep your brain working all morning.

Tips for a healthy diet:

Tips for a healthy diet:

- Eat breakfast! Try adding some raisins or a banana to your cereal.

- Try some raw vegetables as a healthy snack.

- Drink at least one glass of fruit juice a day.

- Drink water regularly to keep the brain hydrated.

- Avoid sugary, carbonated drinks, because they give you a quick buzz and then leave you feeling flat.

- You also need protein, which you can get from eggs, fish, and meat.

Dream machine

Like your body, your brain needs time to rest and recover, so however much you need to prepare for a test, do *not* continue working all night, because you will be exhausted and find it more and more difficult to concentrate the next day. Surprisingly, while you are asleep you brain reprocesses what you have been studying during the day, and you will be amazed at how much easier you remember those things after a good night's sleep.

When you are studying, remember to drink plenty of water to keep your brain hydrated.

Time Management

Once your brain is refreshed and ready to hit the books, the next hurdle is managing your time. Help is at hand, though, and there are a number of strategies you can adopt to get going and see things through to the end.

GET COMFORTABLE!

Arrange your workstation to suit *you!* You may prefer to work in your bedroom or in the living room, or to have your desk in a corner or by a window. Whatever you decide for where you work, make sure that you are comfortable, have enough light, and are sitting comfortably. Finally, keep the equipment you need for your studies close at hand.

Use time efficiently

Time management is an all-important life skill and is the secret of high achievers. If you can master this skill during your school years, you will find it invaluable later in college or in the workplace. Time management requires you to use your time and energy in the most productive manner possible in order to achieve maximum results within a limited time frame.

The key to effective time management lies in breaking lazy habits and in learning to **prioritize** and to overcome **procrastination**. Procrastinators often work long hours, but they spend time doing the wrong tasks. There are a number of reasons why people procrastinate. They may convince themselves that they are waiting for the "right" moment, or they may be perfectionists who are afraid of starting for fear that their work will not be good enough. However, the most common reason for procrastination is feeling that the work is too difficult and that there is too much of it, or that it is something that you do not like doing and you just cannot face it.

It is important that when you take breaks you switch off from your work, so make sure that your "work zone" and "relaxation zone" do not overlap. Don't study on your bed, for example. Your bed is for sleep and relaxation.

TIP

When Alice gets home from school, she is tired and hungry, so she has something to eat and then goes to her desk. She gets out all her books and papers and arranges them neatly. Next she opens her schoolwork diary and thinks, *Math, I can't do that. English, it's a long essay and I can't think where to start. History, we were supposed to write up notes on the discussion we had in class today and I can't remember a thing about it...* Alice suddenly realizes that it is time for her favorite TV show. After watching this she decides to call a friend to see if she can remember anything about the physics experiment. They get talking about weekend plans. Finally, at about 8 p.m., Alice starts to settle down to her schoolwork, by which time she is feeling extremely tired and really not in the right frame of mind to work effectively.

Don't be tempted to start talking with your friends when you should be doing your homework. Wait until you have finished, then call your friends. It will be a reward for all your hard work!

Learn to prioritize

In today's fast-paced society, people regularly complain that they have too much to do and too little time in which to do it. The two-step solution is surprisingly straightforward:

1) Rank tasks in the order of their importance.

2) Leave the less important jobs for later and focus on the more pressing ones first.

Let's say that today is Tuesday. You have math homework due tomorrow (Wednesday), history homework due on Friday, and an English paper due next Monday. What do you do first? Since the math is due tomorrow, you should start with it, leaving the history to follow and the English paper last, possibly for the weekend, when you will have more time to think about it.

Pause for a moment and think about how you approach your studies. You may not want to tackle the task with the highest priority first, but that is what you should do. It is important for you to find ways of tackling the work you need to do first, so you can get to the work that you would rather do or that you find easier.

Music and incentives

Some people find they work better with music in the background, while others prefer complete silence. Do whichever suits you best, but if you do have music on, make sure that it helps with your studies by keeping you relaxed and does not distract you.

To increase your motivation, give yourself something to look forward to. This could be something to eat during your mini-breaks or an outing on the weekend if you do well. You cannot and you should not work nonstop, and you will be amazed at how much better you work when you have something fun planned!

Pace yourself and take breaks

Students frequently complain that they find concentration difficult, and that within a few minutes of sitting down to study, their minds begin to wander. This is not uncommon. Nobody can concentrate indefinitely, and you should not expect to work for hours on end without a break.

Your concentration will vastly improve if you set yourself attainable goals by dividing your work into manageable chunks that you can handle. These work periods should be alternated by regular breaks—say, a five-minute break about every 20 minutes, or whatever you like best.

When you are taking a break, try to do something that will take your mind off your studies.

During breaks, get up and walk around to give your brain and body a rest. If you are hungry, eat a piece of fruit—and don't forget to drink water! If, however, you have not quite finished what you planned during study time, try to complete it before you take your break. You will be rewarded with a sense of achievement, which allows you to enjoy your mini-break without any guilt.

19

Get Together!

You have planned your program, flexed your brain, and can manage your time. Don't forget to look around you, too. There is plenty of help at hand among your family and friends! By reaching out to others, you will get things accomplished more quickly and also feel less stressed.

ASKING FOR HELP

There are a number of different ways to get help with problems and make study time more fun and sociable. The most important rule is: "Never be afraid to ask for help." You can almost guarantee that the other person will be delighted to give you a hand and will benefit just as much as you from working together.

Teachers

Teachers are there to help you. If you cannot understand something or you have lost your notes, stay behind at the end of class and ask if you can come to see your teacher later to figure things out. Also, if you get far behind and your work has piled up, don't wait for your teacher to get annoyed—go and explain the problem. As long as you do not do this too often, your teacher should be understanding.

Getting it Wrong

Do not ask or allow your parents to actually do your work for you, particularly if it is homework that prepares you for an important test. In the long run, it will not help you sort out difficulties or learn anything useful—after all, you will be the one who is sitting alone taking the test. In the case of writing a paper, too much parental input will be regarded as cheating. It is fine to tell your parents what you are doing, though. They can suggest new approaches to the work, as long as the ideas you are writing about are your own.

Help at home

Some young people may feel that their parents nag them over their schoolwork, but there is one guaranteed way to stop the nagging. If you are having difficulties with your studies or if you are feeling stressed about your work, talk to your family about your problems. Very often just talking things through puts problems in perspective and makes things seem easier.

You can also ask family members to help you with your work by testing you. Alternatively, try explaining complicated physics or the plot of a play that you have been studying in class. By doing so, you will find that it sticks better in your mind.

Asking your parents for help with schoolwork is fine—but don't ask them to do it for you.

Getting it
Right

Lucy was having trouble with her work and found it hard to settle down to study in the evening. Her friend Emma seemed to find this easier. Lucy was good at English and Emma was good at math. Lucy's mom suggested that Emma and Lucy become "study buddies." Emma could come over some evenings for dinner, and then she and Lucy could settle down to work together. Lucy and Emma had time to be sociable, but they also helped each other with their schoolwork.

Study buddies

Having a study partner can help you improve your studies. You can talk things through with friends and solve problems, bounce ideas off each other, share your opinions, reinforce any problem areas with role-play activities, and generally help each other out with things that you find difficult.

Remember, however, that it must be a *shared* experience that benefits both sides. It must not end up with just one person doing all the work, because the other person will not learn anything and could also end up feeling stupid. Choose your study buddy carefully—he or she should be someone you can work well with. It is a mistake to work with your best friend if you are likely to spend the whole evening gossiping!

Discussion groups

Different teachers have different styles of teaching, but as you progress through your school career, you will find that teachers may start to introduce discussion groups as a useful learning tool. Discussion groups are extremely valuable because they help you to develop your self-confidence in speaking out in front of other people.

In a discussion group you learn how to listen to others, accept criticism, and express your own opinions. Most importantly, discussion groups will help you to develop your **interpersonal skills**. These are invaluable life skills for getting along with others, both at work and in your social life.

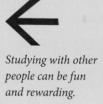

Studying with other people can be fun and rewarding.

QUIZ

STUDY SKILLS

1. **When getting ready for a long study session, do you:**
   a) Take your pen and paper and start immediately?
   b) Rearrange your entire music collection?
   c) Take a look at your calendar and think about what should come first?

2. **When your favorite TV show comes on and you have important work to do, do you:**
   a) Record the show and watch it later?
   b) Watch the show there and then and forget the work until later?
   c) Prioritize your work so you can take a break and watch the show?

3. **When organizing your workspace, do you:**
   a) Clear a corner of the busy sitting room and put on your headphones?
   b) Lie on your bed or clear off the kitchen table whenever you need to work?
   c) Arrange all your work stuff neatly on and around a desk or table in your bedroom?

4. **When you feel tired during study, what should you do?**
   a) Have a mug of tea or coffee.
   b) Go to sleep.
   c) Take a break to drink a glass of water.

5. **When you need some help with your studies, do you:**
   a) Ask a parent or teacher if they can help?
   b) Invite your best friend over and talk all night?
   c) Invite a study buddy over so you can help each other out?

Check page 50 to check your answers.

How Do We Learn?

Educational research has shown that there are three different ways of learning: visual, auditory, and kinesthetic, frequently known as VAK. Each person has his or her own "best" way of learning.

VISUAL LEARNING

Visual learning means learning through sight. It involves the use of pictures, colors, and shapes to help you remember things. Visual aids such as posters, wall displays, and graphic organizers are useful memory aids when following a visual learning approach. Using color or patterns helps people remember important information, too.

Tips for visual learning:

- Use highlighter pens when reading to make important words stand out. Alternatively, you may prefer to underline in pencil, since this can always be erased if you change your mind.

- Use colored index cards for different subjects and use both sides of these cards. For example, write a question on one side and the answer on the other, or write vocabulary in English on one side and in Spanish on the other.

- Use different colored dots for different topics.

- Make **mind maps** or **flowcharts** to help you remember (see pages 32–35).

AUDITORY LEARNING

Auditory learning means learning through listening to noise and sound. People who prefer this method of study are highly sensitive to rhythm and tone. They like to use CDs, DVDs, and videos as a way of remembering things.

Auditory learners can sometimes find it useful to read out loud or move their lips when reading in order to hear the words in their heads. They may also like to listen to recorded information, recite things over to themselves, or make flash cards for specific points and read them out loud to themselves.

Tips for auditory learning:

- Record anything you want to remember onto a tape and listen to your voice. This could be history dates, vocabulary, or even a times table.

- Read things out loud.

- Make up rhymes or stories to help you remember.

- Teach someone else about something you have learned that you want to remember.

- Ask someone to test you on what you have learned.

- Use mind maps and flowcharts to talk through facts and information (see pages 32–35).

Kinesthetic learning

Learning in a kinesthetic way involves the use of feeling and movement in the learning process. People who learn best in this way also tend to experience things on an emotional level. Physical activities, board games, and role-play can all help to imprint things in your memory.

Choosing a method

Practice as many of the VAK learning techniques as you can. They represent the key to successful study by making learning easier, less time consuming, and more effective. While you will probably find that you favor a particular method, it is worth bearing in mind that there are certain tasks that may favor one of the other two styles. An oral exam, for example, would use auditory skills, while a kinesthetic approach may help you with a technology project.

Tips for kinesthetic learning:

- Walk around while studying, and keep moving to help you concentrate.

- Role-play and mime can help make things seem real for you. For example, you could act out a story with a friend or even mime Spanish verbs to help you remember their meaning.

- Be as active as possible. Write things out—several times if necessary. Test yourself and then tear up the paper once you know it.

- Draw up mind maps or flowcharts (see pages 32–35). The process of designing them may help you to remember the detail.

- Make things as real as possible. If you need to know how a medieval castle was built, make a model of the castle.

Experiment to see if one method works better for you than the others. If so, you will find that when you use that method you will be able to remember more accurately what you have read. Planning and writing an essay will become much easier, and you will get much more out of the time you spend studying before tests and exams.

Sharpen your memory

Students frequently complain that they cannot remember what they have studied. This is because they tend to be more aware of the things that they forget (such as irregular verbs in a foreign language) than the things that they remember (such as the rules for football). Your brain takes in much more information than you need, so it is important to identify techniques to help you remember what you actually *need* to know.

There are three important principles to help you improve your memory:

- First, you must *believe* in your ability to retain information.

- Second, you must *understand* what you are trying to remember.

- Third, you need to *organize* your ideas in order to remember them more easily.

Here are some useful methods to help information stick in your memory:

- **Place:** You may associate something with particular surroundings, so think about the place where you studied something.

- **Color:** If you are sensitive to color, you may remember something that you highlighted in a particular color.

- **Personalize it:** Create your own style charts and tables and add the details that you find useful.

- **Mnemonics:** Use memory tricks to help things stick in your brain. For example, use the saying "I before E, except after C" to remember how to spell words like "relieve" and "conceive."

- **Write it down:** When you write things down, it is important to change things into your own words, because this will help to make things stick.

- **Draw it:** Draw and label diagrams, but always make them personal. These could be useful in illustrating processes or concepts.

Left and right brain

People remember things in different ways because the brain has two sides. The left side of the brain is primarily responsible for logical and detailed activities such as reasoning, analysis, and calculation. The right side of the brain involves emotions and imagination. It tends to be more creative and sees the bigger picture.

Though people may find that they favor activities associated with one side of the brain or the other, there is certainly a crossover in our thinking processes as well. It is well worth using a mixture of memory strategies when studying in order to stimulate both sides of the brain.

By reviewing what we have learned at regular intervals, we can prevent the dreaded "memory slide."

The memory slide

Try a mini-experiment by writing down what you remember from a recent class. Then try studying the same topic for over an hour without a break, and again write down what you remember from that class. The parts you will likely remember the best will come from the beginning and end of both your class and your study session.

Concentration tends to run down after a certain period of time, which is why it is essential to take mini-breaks in order to stimulate concentration. In addition, research has shown that we tend to forget most of what we have learned within 24 hours. However, it is possible to counteract this "memory slide" by refreshing our knowledge at regular intervals. This dramatically reduces the percentage of material that we might otherwise forget.

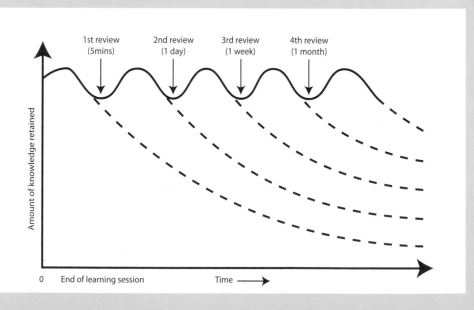

YOUR LEARNING STYLE

1. When reading, do you:
a) Take lots of notes and doodle around the edges of your paper?
b) Read out loud or move your lips to hear the words in your head?
c) Like to walk or move around a lot?

2. How do you best remember things?
a) By picturing them in your mind.
b) By saying them over and over again.
c) By writing them down.

3. When you're at a party, do you:
a) Stand back and watch people?
b) Have a good conversation with someone you find interesting?
c) Join in the dancing and games?

4. If you forget which assignment you should be doing, are you most likely to:
a) Text a friend to ask what needs to be done?
b) Call a friend and find out what it is?
c) Go see a friend and figure it out together?

5. Which of the following are you most likely to do in your free time?
a) Read or watch television.
b) Listen to music.
c) Run or play sports.

6. When explaining something, do you:
a) Write it out?
b) Talk about it?
c) Demonstrate how it works?

Go to page 50 to check your answers.

29

Study Techniques

Try reading a passage from any book, then close the book and jot down what you remember. You will be surprised at how easy it is to forget what you've read, even if you've just read it! How can you improve your ability to retain what you read?

Reading Well

When reading, it is important to read interactively, which means you should think about what you are reading as you read it. Underline keywords, make notes about important points, and use bookmarks or sticky notes so you can easily find useful passages. Remember, though, that if you do not own the book, do not write in it. Make photocopies of important passages instead, or write down the things you know you will need to **reference** again.

Taking notes

As you approach end-of-semester exams, you have to remember things you first learned months before. Learning how to take good notes is essential to this reviewing process. Notes help you to fully understand what you have learned in a class. They help guide you when it comes to remembering all you have learned over the course of the semester. Neat, organized notes will put you in control and make you more positive about your studies.

Shortening words can help you take more efficient notes. Here are some of the abbreviations most commonly used, but you can be creative and invent your own.

e.g. = for example
& = and
yr = year
nb = take note
hr = hour
i.e. = that is to say
> = greater than
< = less than
asap = as soon as possible
∵ = because
∴ = therefore

• CHECKLIST •

- Vary your reading speeds. Read quickly to get a general sense of the passage. Read slowly to understand detailed information.

- If you have a lot to read, take a break to keep your concentration.

- Read aloud to other people and discuss with them what you have read.

- Record certain passages and then listen to them.

- Draw pictures to illustrate the key concepts of what you have read.

- Read a paragraph or short passage two or three times if necessary. Close the book and try to sum up in your own words what you have just read, or write it down if you prefer.

- Write down keywords and main ideas.

- Do not write full sentences.

- Use **abbreviations**.

- Use headings, and number your points.

- Highlight points with different colors.

- Use diagrams, pictures, arrows, and circles to link up your ideas. Use mind maps and flowcharts (see pages 32–35).

- Keep notes neat by using files and dividers so you can find things easily.

Asking small children to read out loud is one of the keys to improving their reading skills.

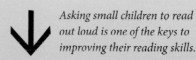

MAKING A MIND MAP

Mind maps are charts that use color, pictures, keywords, and groups of words and ideas. They are adaptable and can provide you with a lot of help and support in any or all of the following situations: taking notes in class, summarizing what you have read, writing an essay, and studying for tests or exams.

Let's look at an example. Read the following passage about dragonflies.

*Dragonflies, like all insects, have bodies that are divided into three basic parts: the head with **multifaceted** eyes, the thorax to which the four wings and six legs are attached, and the abdomen, with its 10 segments.*

*Dragonflies are **agile** insects and can hover, glide, fly forward, backward, and sideways. They can quickly change direction and speed.*

The life cycle of a dragonfly lasts between one and two years and is mostly spent underwater. Eggs are laid in underwater plants, the mud, or directly in the water of rivers or ponds. When the eggs hatch out into larvae, they shed their skin while growing to full size and developing "wing buds." When fully grown, the larvae climb out of the water onto leaves or twigs, their skin splits, and the young adults emerge and fly away. They will not generally return to the water until they are ready to mate.

You can create a mind map by first underlining, highlighting, or writing down the keywords, and then creating a diagram that links those keywords together.

The keywords are:

insect / three parts / head - eyes / thorax - wings & legs / abdomen - segments / agile / flies forward & backward / changes direction / life cycle / eggs underwater / mud / pond / larvae / sheds skins / leaves water / flies away / returns to mate

You then use the keywords to build your mind map, linking together the various bits of information as illustrated on the opposite page. Don't worry about using full sentences to do this. You are just getting all the key points down on paper so that you can expand on them later.

Using a mind map to illustrate the life cycle of the dragonfly makes it much easier to remember the essential facts about the insect.

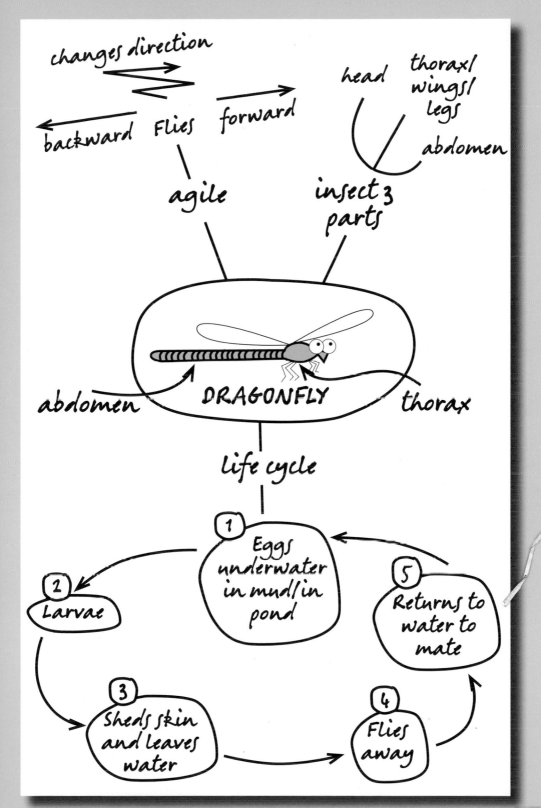

MAKING A FLOWCHART

Some students prefer to use flowcharts, which are useful if you need to remember a sequence. They can be used to remember the order of events or things, or they can be used in a literary context, such as the plot of a play. To show how a flowchart works, let's look at William Shakespeare's *Romeo and Juliet*.

The outline of the plot is as follows:

The play is set in Verona, in Italy, where the two main families, the Montagues [Romeo's family] and the Capulets [Juliet's family], have argued for years.

Romeo's friends smuggle him into a party at the Capulets' house, where he meets Juliet. Romeo and Juliet fall in love, but then realize that their families are enemies. Romeo later climbs over the walls of the Capulets' garden. Juliet's window opens onto the garden, so they talk, but Juliet has to go because her nurse arrives. Romeo leaves and asks his friend Friar Lawrence to marry them. Romeo and Juliet marry in secret.

Juliet's cousin Tybalt kills Romeo's friend Mercutio. In a fit of rage, Romeo kills Tybalt and is banished to Mantua. Juliet's father arranges for her to marry Paris, a Capulet. Juliet asks Friar Lawrence for help. He gives her a potion that will make her look as though she is dead. Romeo hears the news that Juliet is dead, *so, not knowing the truth, he goes to see Juliet for one last time and kills himself with poison. Juliet wakes to find Romeo lying dead next to her. In despair, she takes his dagger and kills herself by stabbing herself in the chest. After seeing their children's dead bodies, the Capulets and Montagues agree to end their long-standing* **feud**.

The key ideas are:

Montagues – Romeo / Capulets – Juliet / families argue / Capulet party / Romeo & Juliet meet – fall in love / families enemies / Capulets garden – Romeo and Juliet talk/ Friar Lawrence – marriage / Romeo kills Tybalt – banished / Juliet to marry Paris/ Friar Lawrence helps – potion to seem dead / Romeo believes Juliet dead / Romeo poisons self / Juliet kills self

Now try creating a flowchart for *Romeo and Juliet* using the model shown on page 35.

Planning an essay, and in particular making sure that your arguments are properly illustrated and lead to a logical conclusion, is much easier with the help of a flowchart.

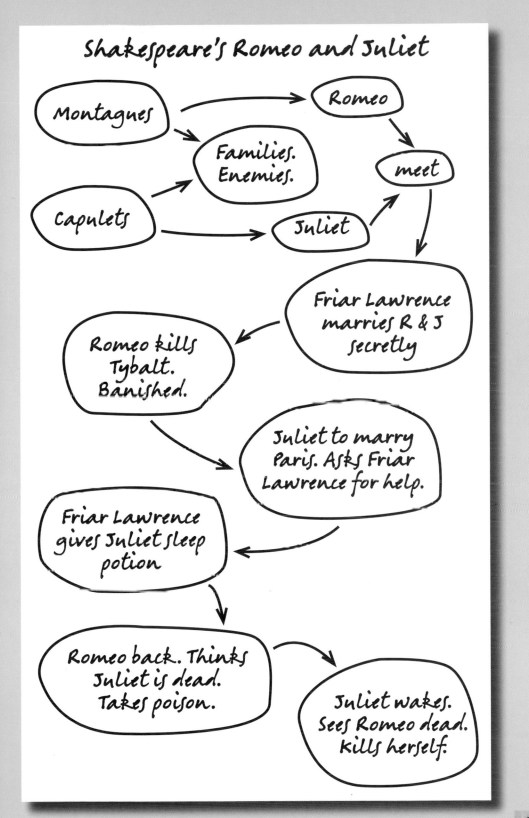

Shakespeare's Romeo and Juliet

Montagues → Romeo

Montagues → Families. Enemies.

Capulets → Families. Enemies.

Capulets → Juliet

Romeo → meet

Juliet → meet

meet → Friar Lawrence marries R & J secretly

Friar Lawrence marries R & J secretly → Romeo kills Tybalt. Banished.

Romeo kills Tybalt. Banished. → Juliet to marry Paris. Asks Friar Lawrence for help.

Juliet to marry Paris. Asks Friar Lawrence for help. → Friar Lawrence gives Juliet sleep potion

Friar Lawrence gives Juliet sleep potion → Romeo back. Thinks Juliet is dead. Takes poison.

Romeo back. Thinks Juliet is dead. Takes poison. → Juliet wakes. Sees Romeo dead. Kills herself.

Essay Writing and Project Work

One of the most difficult things with any project, whether it is connected to schoolwork, housework, or exercise, is *getting started!* This is particularly true of essay writing and project work. However, there are some simple steps you can follow to take the sting out of getting going.

The Big Idea

Brainstorming is a technique you can use whenever you are faced with a project and do not know where to start. Take a piece of paper and write down any ideas as fast as you can. Next, write down all the questions that you can possibly think of in relation to the topic, asking "who, what, where, when, why, and how." This will get your mind buzzing with ideas.

Review your ideas and consider which would be the best to follow through with, or try discussing your ideas with someone else. It is useful to have other people's opinions, because they can trigger fresh ideas.

Put your ideas into some form of order by using index cards or cutting up small bits of cardboard and jotting down notes on each card. Use different colored cards to split up the main sections. Highlight the main points and additional ideas using different colors, and number your points using numbers and letters.

Lastly, build up a **spidergram** linking all your ideas. A spidergram has the same design as a mind map, but is slightly more **random**, because at this stage you are just exploring all possible approaches.

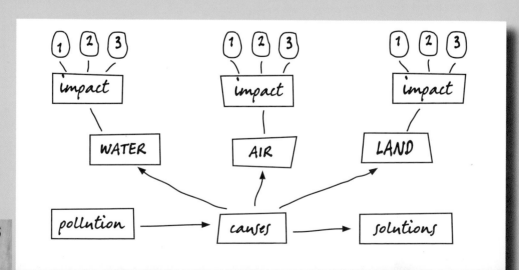

Research

Frequently, you will be asked to write an essay or do a project that requires getting hold of some background information. In these cases you will need to do some research. Researching a topic may involve any or all of the following:

- Reading books, magazines, and journals

- Using the Internet

- Doing fieldwork, such as exploring something in your local community

- Interviewing people

Author's purpose

Think about the purpose of your essay. Every author has a purpose including you.

If your assignment asks you to express an opinion on something, think about what your opinion is and describe it in your essay. If the assignment asks you just to describe or inform, then remain neutral and avoid offering an opinion on your topic.

Think about what *exactly* you have been asked to write about. Before you begin, make sure that you completely understand the assignment and what you have to do to complete it. When you receive an assignment, first highlight the keywords in it. Then think about each of these words, starting with the easiest before moving on to more difficult keywords. Think about which keyword you know most about. Start your essay by brainstorming what you know about that keyword. Then move on to the other keywords.

A spidergram encourages you to think of how ideas can link up, which will help you to form logical arguments. This spidergram outlines the ideas you might use for a project on environmental pollution.

LIBRARY BASICS

Public libraries can be found everywhere, and membership is free and open to all. If you want to check out books and you do not have a library card, you will have to apply for one. Check what is required with your local library, but you will probably need a form of identification. You may also need a parent or guardian's signature and proof of their address.

Once you have joined the library, find out a few useful bits of information:

- How many books can you check out at a time?
- How long can you keep books out?
- Are there any fines?
- Can you reserve or renew books by telephone or online?

DID YOU KNOW?

If you think your local library is big, try this on for size! The Library of Congress, located in Washington, D.C., contains more than 138 million items, including books, recordings, photographs, maps, and manuscripts. It is the largest library in the world. To hold its collections, the library has about 650 miles (1,050 kilometers) of bookshelves!

• CHECKLIST •

What is in a library?

- Books, divided into fiction and nonfiction
- Catalogs [of books]; these may be on card, microfiche, CD Rom, or computer
- Local and community information
- Magazines and newspapers
- CDs, tapes, and slides
- DVDs and videos
- Music and movies
- Photocopiers
- Computers with Internet access and word-processing programs
- Tables for quiet study or reading

Getting help

When preparing to write about a specific topic, you can start by visiting your local library and asking a librarian to help. He or she will be able to show you where to find the books you need and will probably be able to offer some suggestions. Librarians arrange reference books by subject, so that you will see a number of different books on the same topic in the same place.

If you know what you need to find, check before you go to see if your local library has its catalog available online. You can use keywords and an online catalog to search for books in much the same way that you can use keywords and a search engine to search for websites.

If you cannot find what you are looking for in your local library, try searching for it in other libraries. A handy search facility, available at **www.worldcat.org**, allows you to search all the libraries in the country or even the world—or you can focus your search so that you only look at libraries closer to home.

Once you have all the books you need for your research, you will feel empowered and ready for action!

DO YOUR RESEARCH

Once you have found your resources, it is time to get focused! As you review sources, look out for keywords that relate to your topic. Take notes to record relevant information, keeping track of the source and pages number. Don't forget to put quotation marks around any text that you take down **verbatim**.

If you find that an entire page or chapter would be useful to your essay but you cannot check out that particular reference book, then make photocopies.

Fieldwork

Gathering information from the big wide world can be fun! Fieldwork gets you out and away from sitting in front of books or at a computer. But, as with the Internet, use it carefully. Stay with your group and do not wander off anywhere on your own.

Before you set out, figure out precisely what you are looking for. Create an action plan that clearly states your objective and the step-by-step process you hope to follow. Planning ahead will help you be organized when you actually get to the site of your fieldwork. An example of fieldwork might involve going to a museum for a history project or going to a beach for a geography project.

Getting it Wrong

Plagiarism is copying other people's thoughts and ideas without putting these into your own words or adding your own opinion. Copying passages word-for-word from the Internet or from books is a *very dangerous practice*. Teachers will immediately recognize work that is not your own and will not accept it. If you plagiarize in a paper or on a test you might be given a failing grade. Plagiarism is always considered bad practice, and in some cases it may even be illegal. If you do need to quote from a source, use quotation marks, indent the passage quoted, and make a note of where it comes from. Later, in college, you will be expected to list your sources at the end of each paper. It is a good thing to get into this habit as early as possible.

Interviewing people

Again, careful preparation pays off when you interview someone for an essay or report. As with fieldwork, figure out precisely what you are looking for before you set out. How many people do you need to interview? What questions do you plan on asking them? Research as much as you can before you interview someone, so that the questions you ask are useful.

For example, if you are looking for a quote to put in an essay, you probably do not want to ask questions for which the possible answers are just "yes" or "no." However, if you are taking a poll and want to tally up how many people feel one way or another, you do not want your interviewees going on and on about their opinions. A simple "yes" or "no" answer will work!

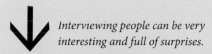

Interviewing people can be very interesting and full of surprises.

Getting it Right

Always follow these rules when doing fieldwork or interviewing people:

- Ask permission from your parents or guardian before leaving.

- Work in pairs or take an adult with you.

- Make sure people know where you are and when you are expected back.

- Take a cell phone, and make sure you have a signal.

- Stay in well-populated areas and do not go out after dark without an adult.

Tests and Exams

Exams and tests are very much like important games in sports. Life without exams and tests would be like playing soccer or tennis and never playing in an actual match. You would cruise along, but you never raise your game and put your skills to the test.

STAYING POSITIVE

When taking exams, the first word of advice is to remain positive. Treat exams as a challenge that offers you the opportunity to demonstrate that you have worked hard and mastered the subject matter.

Success depends on your mindset. Compare yourself to a top sports star prior to a competition or a game. Having undergone a rigorous training program, you are in peak condition and are ready to have your skills tested.

Skills and strategies

During the important pre-exam study period, you will be employing all the study skill strategies you have been practicing throughout the semester. Before you begin your studies, look back briefly at the techniques that have been discussed in earlier chapters to remind yourself which of these you found most useful.

Use a combination of study skills, such as visual, audible, and kinesthetic learning aids, mind maps, or flowcharts. This will help you review different aspects of the class. A visual example is putting up Post-It™ notes around your bedroom for vocabulary review.

Overall planning

Find out the dates and times of your exams and draw up a study timetable. Put these dates and times on your wall chart or in your diary. Plan to work hard each day and establish a realistic routine you can follow. Apart from allowing time for rest and relaxation, allow some extra time in case you need it, since things often take longer than you think. Be flexible and prepared to change plans if necessary. You may find that you work better at certain times of the day.

Let others close to you know about your plans—both family and friends—so you have a support network ready to help you out if you need them.

Getting it
Wrong

Without a plan, you will get into trouble. If you just try to "push forward," working all day, you will get too tired and will not be able to concentrate. If you try to cram information into your head at the last minute, particularly immediately before an exam, it won't stick—and it can easily prove counterproductive by messing up what you have already learned. Finally, don't be too rigid with your plan. You may find that on some days you need to change it, so don't get upset if you find you cannot always do as much as you had hoped.

Libraries are quiet places where you can study uninterrupted. Checking out the books can also give you lots of ideas.

Getting focused

First, identify the most important topics you have studied in your class and those that are most likely to come up on your exam. Make sure, with help from a teacher if necessary, that you sort out any problem areas you think you may face on the exam.

Make sure that you are familiar with the format of each exam that you will be taking:

- How long will the exam last?

- How many questions do you have to answer?

- What is the desired length for answers to essay questions?

- Are there any multiple-choice questions?

- What tools are you allowed to use? For instance, are you allowed to use a calculator, and, if so, what kind?

- Are you allowed to use a dictionary?

- Is it an "open book" exam? If so, what texts are you allowed to bring in?

Pay attention in class or ask your teacher if you do not know the answers to any of these questions.

Pick and mix

When studying, try to mix easy and difficult topics, and things that you find more interesting and less interesting. This will help you with the

Getting it Wrong

Don't waste your precious time! For example:

- Don't waste time on minor topics that are unlikely to come up.

- Don't waste time going over things that you know already.

- Don't waste time memorizing things that will be available to you if the test is "open book."

- Don't spend hours and hours on one subject and forget to do the others.

- Don't just read things through without questioning what you are reading.

- Don't spend hours carefully recopying your notes. This will not help you remember them.

problem areas and keep you alert. If you are studying something you do not particularly enjoy, follow it up with a topic you prefer.

No matter what you are studying, try to study in an active way. Make a list of key points and test your memory as you go along. If you have trouble remembering things such as dates or math formulas, post them up around your room so that you see them all the time.

Building up

In the last days leading up to a big exam, do not forget to eat well, get plenty of sleep, and drink water. Give yourself little treats to reward yourself when you do well or achieve a deadline. Don't forget to keep thinking positively. Tell yourself that you are prepared for the exam and that you will do well.

Spend your free time out and about having fun with friends rather than slumped in front of the television. Socialize with people who are upbeat, positive thinkers, rather than hanging around people who are feeling overwhelmed or depressed. Their mood might make positive thinking more difficult. Never say that you are not good at something.

As you study, keep yourself in good physical shape by getting plenty of exercise.

KEY INFORMATION

Make sure that you know the meaning of any words that might come up in standard questions, such as *discuss*, *define*, *analyze*, *compare and contrast*, or *summarize*. In the case of a foreign language exam, in which the instructions are given in that language, make sure that you know the meaning of the words commonly used. Ask your teacher if you are unsure of some of these words.

Exam day

On the morning of an exam, give yourself extra time to get ready for the day. Eat a well-balanced breakfast. When you sit down to your exam, take a deep breath and then get started!

Essay exams

When tackling an essay question, follow the same process for creating a mind map or flowchart. Before answering an essay question, underline keywords, make notes, and draw up a plan. When you are ready to put pen or pencil to paper, start with a short introduction, followed by the main body of your argument and then a conclusion.

• CHECKLIST •

Top tips…for exam day:

- Read each question through slowly and carefully before deciding on the answer. Be sure to read any instructions on the page.

- If you are given a choice of questions, read them all through before deciding which ones you can do best.

- Figure out how much time you will have for each question and keep your eye on the time.

- Stay calm. If you do panic and your mind goes blank, put your pen down, sit still, and breathe deeply. This should help you to relax so that your brain gets back into gear.

- If you run out of time and you find that you cannot finish your last question, write notes. If these are relevant, the teacher will probably give some credit.

Multiple-choice exams

Read through multiple-choice
questions carefully, since misreading
can easily lead you to choose an
incorrect answer. If you are stuck, do
not waste time. Just keep going. Do
the easiest questions first and then
go on to the more difficult ones. If
you change your mind, make sure you
erase the mark in the wrong box, so
that only the box you think is correct
is marked. Unless there are penalties
for incorrect answers (always check
first), you should always take a guess,
after narrowing down your choices as
far as possible.

Oral exams

Foreign language exams are often
oral. They are designed to test your
knowledge and understanding of
the language and your ability to
communicate in that language. Before
exam day, make sure you know what
form the exam will take. It may be
a list of questions or an informal
discussion, or both. Get plenty of
practice, perferably in "mock" exam
conditions, because this is the best
way to overcome nerves when it
comes to the real exam.

*Once you get started,
you won't find
concentrating on your
exam a problem.*

AFTER THE EXAM

Exams are just one of the many hurdles that you have to overcome in the course of your school career. Don't blow things out of proportion—an exam is just a means to an end and not an end in itself! If you have done well, that is a good excuse for a celebration. You deserve to enjoy yourself after all your hard work.

If, as is sometimes the case, you have not done as well as you might have hoped, use the experience as a learning opportunity. Ask your teacher to go through your results with you, so that you can see how you can improve in the future. The chances are that you will know where you went wrong. Don't get depressed—move on, learn from your mistakes, hold your head high, and face the next challenge. It won't be long before it arrives!

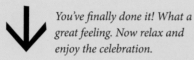

You've finally done it! What a great feeling. Now relax and enjoy the celebration.

TAKING TESTS

1. When taking notes, do you:
a) Scribble gossip down on a piece of paper to hand to a friend?
b) Include as much detail as possible in full sentences?
c) Note keywords and main ideas using abbreviations?

2. When making a mind map or flowchart, do you:
a) Try to figure out the distance between related concepts?
b) Highlight keywords and imagine how they are interconnected?
c) Highlight any keywords and then interconnect them in a chart?

3. What are you most likely to do in the days before a major exam?
a) Chill out and watch television to relax.
b) Rewrite notes over and over again and study nonstop.
c) Get plenty of sleep, eat well, exercise, drink water, and keep up your study routine.

4. How would you most likely approach an essay exam?
a) Start writing your answer right away.
b) Look for the keywords and try to think about what they mean.
c) Underline the keywords and write notes. Draw a mind map showing that you have understood their meaning and how you can use mind maps to plan your essay.

5. What do you do if you don't do well on an exam?
a) Get depressed.
b) Tell yourself that it is not your fault.
c) Recognize where the problems may have occurred and move on.

Go to page 50 to check your answers.

STUDY SKILLS
For page 23

If you mostly answered:

a) You have passed! Your study skills aren't bad, but could use some fine tuning.

b) You've flunked! You need to rethink how to approach your studies in order to complete them well and on time.

c) You have aced it! You have solid study skills and prioritize well.

TAKING TESTS
For page 49

If you mostly answered:

a) You are not prepared for the exam. Time to review the pages of this book again—in greater detail!

b) You are a hard worker, but still have some way to go to improve your test-taking skills.

c) Most times, you are ready for the exam. You have learned how to approach exams positively and successfully.

YOUR LEARNING STYLE
For page 29

If you mostly answered:

a) You are a visual learner. See the big picture and use visual aids to help you remember things better.

b) You are an auditory learner. Listen to your mind and use audio aids to help you remember things better.

c) You are a kinesthetic learner. Use motion and touch to help you remember things better.

ANSWER TO RIDDLE
on page 12

Sunglasses

(They sit on the BRIDGE of your nose!)

20 THINGS TO REMEMBER

1. Start the school year organized—and remain organized throughout.

2. Drink plenty of water and eat a healthy diet.

3. Get plenty of fresh air and exercise.

4. Create a comfortable workstation for yourself.

5. Get into the habit of prioritizing your work.

6. Don't procrastinate!

7. Pace yourself, taking breaks at regular intervals.

8. Never be afraid to ask for help.

9. Be prepared to accept criticism and advice from your teachers.

10. Practice different learning strategies and use whichever suits you best.

11. Be flexible in your approach to your studies.

12. Review and recall what you have learned at regular intervals.

13. Read in an active manner.

14. Practice doing mind maps and flowcharts.

15. Use the Internet intelligently and not as a time waster.

16. Never plagiarize!

17. Avoid people who think they will fail or who do not want to work.

18. Before answering a question on an exam, underline keywords and make sure that you are answering the question, not just writing down everything you know about the topic.

19. If you do not do as well as hoped on an exam, use it as a learning experience to help you to do better in the future.

20. Stay positive and maintain your will to achieve your goals.

Further Information

BOOKS/GUIDES

Frender, Gloria. *Learning to Learn: Strengthening Study Skills and Brain Power*. Nashville: Incentive, 2004.

How to Study for Success. Hoboken, N.J.: J. Wiley & Sons, 2004.

Kesselman-Turkel, Judi. *Note-Taking Made Easy*. Madison: University of Wisconsin Press, 2003.

Moss, Samantha, and Lesley Schwartz. *Where's My Stuff? The Ultimate Teen Organizing Guide*. San Francisco: Zest, 2007.

Rozakis, Laurie. *Super Study Skills: The Ultimate Guide to Tests and Studying*. New York: Scholastic, 2002.

WEBSITES

The Library of Congress
www.loc.gov
Visit the website of the Library of Congress, which is full of information, including online catalogs, information, and exhibitions.

Calendar Home
www.calendarhome.com
Print out a blank calendar for any month in any year so that you can organize upcoming events.

WorldCat
www.worldcat.org
Use this helpful guide to library collections throughout the United States and the world.

Google Calendar
www.google.com/calendar
Stay organized by creating a schedule that you can view by day, week, or month. You can even share it with family or friends.

How-To-Study.com
www.how-to-study.com
Learn more about the study skills you can apply in different areas.

Institute of Education Sciences: Library Statistics Program
http://nces.ed.gov/surveys/libraries/librarysearch/
Find your local library.

Xdrive
www.xdrive.com
Store computer files here and access them from any computer, or simply backup your files for free.

Glossary

abbreviation shortened form of a word or phrase, consisting of a letter or group of letters taken from the word

agile quick or nimble

brainstorming jotting down any sudden idea you have about a topic

feud long-standing, bitter argument, especially between families

flowchart similar to a mind map, a flowchart is a diagram that connects keywords and ideas in a downward and sideways format

glucose simple sugar found in the blood that is the main source of energy for the body

interpersonal skills ability to form harmonious relationships with people around you by being sensitive to their character, mood, and situation

irrelevant not important or relevant

ISP Internet Service Provider

mind map diagram that uses color, pictures, and keywords in a spiral format to help a learner understand and remember key points of a particular topic and how they are linked

mnemonics words, letters, symbols, abbreviations, techniques, or devices used to help people remember things

multifaceted something that has more than one or two sides

nervous system body system that consists of the brain, the spinal cord, and additional nerves that branch off from the spinal cord

neuron cell that receives and sends messages from the body to the brain, and back to the body

nutrient chemical that is needed by plants and animals for growth and development

plagiarism use someone else's written, artistic, musical, or scientific ideas and pretend that they are your own

prioritize deal with things, events, or people in order of importance or value

procrastination act of putting off or avoiding doing something for no good reason

psychologist professional who practices psychology, the study of thought and behavior

puberty time of life when a child gradually changes into an adult. This can start any time between the ages of 11 and 18.

random with no definite order

reference look at or look up; also, an information source

riddle puzzle using words

spidergram early version of a mind map that contains random thoughts

stimulate encourage

synonym word that has the same meaning as the one you are trying to use

thesaurus reference book that lists words and their synonyms or related words

time management planning and making efficient and effective use of the time available for any given project

tracking editing facility in word-processing software that allows you to see what corrections have been made to a piece of text

trivia unimportant or insignificant fact

verbatim repeating something using exactly the same words

Index